D1369422

SNOW LEOPARDS

BY PATRICIA HUTCHISON

The Child's World

Published by The Child's World®
1980 Lookout Drive • Mankato, MN 56003-1705
800-599-READ • www.childsworld.com

Acknowledgments
The Child's World®: Mary Berendes, Publishing Director
Red Line Editorial: Editorial direction and production
The Design Lab: Design
Amnet: Production

Design Element: Shutterstock Images
Photographs ©: Abeselom Zerit/Shutterstock Images, cover,
1; iStockphoto, 4, 10, 13, 21; Shutterstock Images, 6–7,
16, 22; Christian Schoissingeyer/Shutterstock Images, 8;
Dennis W. Donohue/Shutterstock Images, 11; Jeannette
Katzir Photog/Shutterstock Images, 15; Frans Lanting/Corbis
Images, 17; Lizette Potgieter/Shutterstock Images, 18-19

Copyright © 2016 by The Child's World®
All rights reserved. No part of this book may be reproduced
or utilized in any form or by any means without written
permission from the publisher.

ISBN 9781631439742
LCCN 2014959642

Printed in the United States of America
Mankato, MN
July, 2015
PA02264

ABOUT THE AUTHOR

A former teacher, Patricia Hutchison is a lover of nature. She enjoys watching and learning about all kinds of wildlife. Birds, fish, mammals, and even certain species of amphibians and insects fascinate her. Hutchison enjoys writing books for children about science and nature.

TABLE OF CONTENTS

CHAPTER ONE

DRESSED FOR THE COLD

**Warm fur and big paws help snow leopards
live in cold, snowy areas.**

The snow leopard wraps its long tail around its body like a
winter scarf. Its thick fur keeps it warm in its cold mountain
home. The cat's large, furry paws work like snowshoes. They
keep the wild cat from sinking into the deep snow. Its wide,

short nose warms the air coming into its body. This cat is designed to stay warm in the bitter cold.

Snow leopards live in central Asia. They are found in China and 11 other countries. These wild cats live on steep, rocky mountain slopes. They walk easily on the edges of cliffs. These cliffs can be more than 10,000 feet (3,048 m) high. That high, the air is cold and dry. Trees cannot live there. Only grasses and small shrubs can grow.

The snow leopard's fur helps it blend in with its **habitat**. Its fur is white with black-and-brown spots. Snow leopards are about 3 to 4 feet (0.9 to 1.2 m) long. They have tails that can be 40 inches (1 m) long. They are approximately 2 feet (0.6 m) tall. The cats weigh between 77 and 121 pounds (35 and 55 kg).

HEAR ME YOWL!

Unlike other big cats, snow leopards cannot roar. Instead they hiss, growl, and yowl. More often, snow leopards make a happier-sounding noise. It is a loud puffing sound called a chuff. They can even purr like housecats.

Though smaller than many other big cats, snow leopards are powerful. They can leap up to 30 feet (9 m). That is almost six times the length of their bodies. This makes them excellent hunters. They feed on blue sheep and **ibex**. Snow leopards eat **hares** and game birds, too. A snow leopard can take a few days to finish its meal. The cat must hunt every eight to ten days. Sometimes there are no wild animals to hunt.

It is difficult to spot a snow leopard in its rocky habitat.

Sure-footed ibex can be difficult for
snow leopards to hunt.

Instead a snow leopard might kill sheep, goats, or horses that

belong to people. Snow leopards also eat grass and twigs.

Scientists believe the plants help keep the cats healthy.

Healthy adult female snow leopards have two or three

cubs at a time. At two months, the cubs can eat solid food.

They learn to hunt once they are a few months old. Their mothers provide food and shelter until they are one to two years old. Snow leopards live up to 12 years in the wild.

At the age of two, a snow leopard leaves its mother. It lives by itself in its **territory**. This territory may be 50 to 60 square miles (129 to 155 sq km). The leopard scratches and

Snow leopards take a few years to grow
to their adult size.

male
female

baby cub

2 months

3 months

18–24 months

2–4 years

adult

scrapes the ground. These marks tell other snow leopards that the territory is taken. Adult snow leopards usually hide from other animals and people. People sometimes call them "gray ghosts" or "ghost cats." This behavior makes it hard for scientists to study snow leopards.

Shy snow leopards are difficult for scientists to study.

CHAPTER TWO

THREATS TO SNOW LEOPARDS

Snow leopard numbers are decreasing.

Today scientists estimate that there are fewer than 2,500 wild snow leopards left. They are **endangered**. Humans are their biggest threat.

Human activities can harm these big cats. Sometimes snow leopards kill farmers' animals. This angers farmers and makes them lose food and money. They poison or shoot the snow leopards. This has caused a steep drop in snow leopard numbers. To make more money, the farmers increase the size of their herds. More farm animals eat more grass. Ibex have less grass to eat. They die off. Then the snow leopards have less food to eat.

Poachers are another threat to snow leopards. They hunt snow leopards to make money. The cat's fur is popular. People use it to make expensive coats. Body parts are used as a kind of medicine in parts of Asia. Some cats are captured as pets. Because snow leopards live in such rough territory, it is easy for poachers to hide. Police have trouble catching the criminals.

MONEY MAKERS

Many people who live near snow leopards make less than $300 each year. A poacher can sell a single dead snow leopard for $200. The buyer can then sell the animal again for more than $10,000. This is a major reason why snow leopards are endangered.

Some people use snow leopard fur to make coats for humans.

Mining is another activity that threatens snow leopards. Miners use dangerous chemicals. They also use explosives. This causes a lot of harm to snow leopard habitat. The snow leopards and their prey must find other places to live.

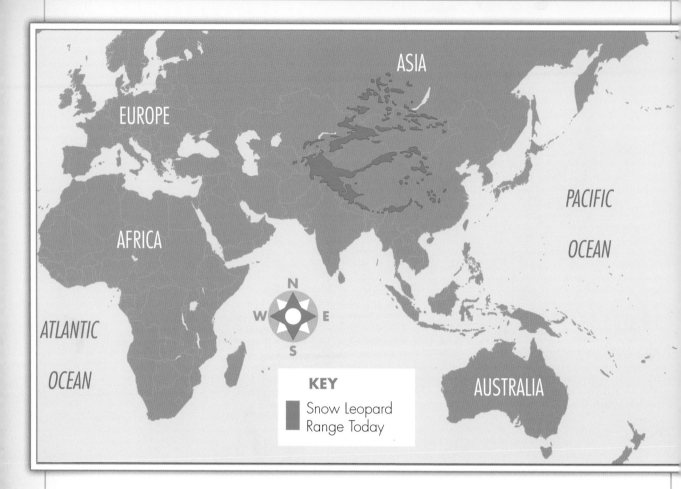

Snow leopards live in central Asia.

Climate change also threatens snow leopards. Temperatures rise, making the snow leopard's habitat warmer. Snow is found farther up on the mountains. Higher up, plants do not grow well. It is hard for plant eaters to survive. Snow leopards hunt these plant eaters. When they do not survive, snow leopards have trouble finding food.

Scientists who study snow leopards believe the cats are in trouble. They may become **extinct** if not helped.

Scientists think snow leopards could become extinct.

CHAPTER THREE

HELPING SNOW LEOPARDS

With human help, these snow leopard cubs may
grow up to have cubs of their own.

Today many people work to help snow leopard numbers grow.

Some efforts focus on helping the cats. Others help educate

the people who may think about killing a snow leopard.

People in Pakistan created parks and **preserves** to

protect snow leopards. Afghanistan also created protected

areas for snow leopards, blue sheep, and ibex. The World **Conservation** Society works with people to manage these protected areas. The Snow Leopard Conservancy uses cameras to spot snow leopards. These cameras take pictures of animals that pass by. Computers count and track the snow leopards. There is no need to capture or mark them. The cats can be studied more easily.

Camera traps such as this one help scientists study snow leopards.

Snow leopards sometimes prey on the animals people raise. The Snow Leopard Project helps farmers. It pays them for animals snow leopards kill. It also spends money to make safe livestock pens. Farmers are now less likely to kill the cats that hunt their animals. This has helped snow leopard numbers remain the same and even grow.

Disease is a major threat to the herders' flocks. To help, the Snow Leopard Trust began **vaccinating** animals in

Farmers in Afghanistan vaccinate their livestock so more survive.

Afghanistan and Pakistan. If there is less disease, the people can raise more livestock. One animal killed by a snow leopard is no longer a big loss.

There is one problem with this, though. Larger herds eat more grass. This means ibex and sheep have less to eat. This means less food for the snow leopards. Farmers must agree to limit the number of animals they raise. If they do not, their animals are not vaccinated. This agreement is good for both the people and the snow leopards. The people can make more money. Snow leopards have enough to eat.

The Snow Leopard Trust trains people to make products from the wool of their livestock. The trust also provides the needed equipment. People sell rugs, hats, gloves, and other products to the trust. The money helps them make a better living. They are able to buy the food, medicine, and clothing

USING FIRE

Long ago, Pakistani farmers used fire to scare away snow leopards. The fires blazed all day and night. The cats stayed away. As a result, there is very little firewood left. The farmers are unable to build fires. Instead some use guns to keep their animals safe.

With human help, snow leopards can continue to
hunt, play, and roll in their snowy habitat.

they need. The trust sells their products online. The money the
trust makes goes back to conservation programs.

Before people start working with the Snow Leopard Trust,
everyone must make a promise. They must promise not to
poach snow leopards. If they do not poach the cats, they get
more money. But if a snow leopard is killed, no one gets any
money. This encourages people to work together to protect
snow leopards. Working together, people can help increase
the number of these beautiful, wild cats.

WHAT YOU CAN DO

- Share things you learn about snow leopards and other endangered animals. If more people know about snow leopards, more will want to help the wild cats.

- Many zoos are home to endangered animals. Volunteer with an adult at a zoo.

- Organize a fundraiser for snow leopards. Have a bake sale, yard sale, or car wash. Give the money to an organization that helps save snow leopards.

GLOSSARY

climate change (KLI-mit CHANJ) Climate change is a term for significant, long-term changes in Earth's temperature, wind patterns, and rain and snowfall totals. Climate change affects snow leopard habitat.

conservation (kon-sur-VAY-shun) Conservation is the protection of animals, plants, and their habitats. Some conservation groups protect snow leopards.

endangered (en-DANE-jerd) An endangered animal is in danger of becoming extinct. Snow leopards are endangered.

extinct (ek-STINKT) If a type of animal is extinct, all the animals have died out. Snow leopards may become extinct.

habitat (HAB-i-tat) A habitat is a place where an animal lives. Mountains in Asia are snow leopard habitat.

hares (HAYRS) Hares are mammals that are like large rabbits, with strong rear legs. Snow leopards eat hares.

ibex (EYE-beks) Ibex are wild goats that live in the mountains of Asia. Snow leopards eat ibex.

poachers (PO-churz) Poachers are people who illegally hunt and kill animals. Poachers kill snow leopards for their fur.

preserves (pree-ZURVZ) Preserves are places where plants, animals, and other natural things are protected. Some snow leopards live in preserves.

territory (TER-eh-tor-ee) A territory is an area of land that an animal controls as its own. An adult snow leopard protects its territory.

vaccinating (VAK-suh-nate-ing) When vaccinating an animal, it is given medicine to prevent disease. Farmers get help vaccinating their animals.

TO LEARN MORE

BOOKS

Esbaum, Jill. *Snow Leopards*. Washington, DC:
National Geographic Society, 2014.

Montgomery, Sy. *Saving the Ghost of the Mountain:
An Expedition among Snow Leopards in Mongolia*. Boston:
Houghton Mifflin Books for Children, 2009.

Rose, Naomi C. *Where Snow Leopard Prowls: Wild Animals
of Tibet*. Sedona, AZ: Dancing Dakini Press, 2012.

WEB SITES

Visit our Web site for links about snow leopards:
childsworld.com/links

*Note to Parents, Teachers, and Librarians: We routinely verify our Web links to make
sure they are safe and active sites. So encourage your readers to check them out!*

INDEX